Cambridge Plain Texts

LANCELOT ANDREWES
TWO SERMONS

T0349130

LANCELOT ANDREWES

TWO SERMONS
OF THE
RESURRECTION

CAMBRIDGE
AT THE UNIVERSITY PRESS
1932

CAMBRIDGE UNIVERSITY PRESS
Cambridge, New York, Melbourne, Madrid, Cape Town,
Singapore, São Paulo, Delhi, Mexico City

Cambridge University Press
The Edinburgh Building, Cambridge CB2 8RU, UK

Published in the United States of America by Cambridge University Press, New York

www.cambridge.org
Information on this title: www.cambridge.org/9781107690394

First published 1932
Re-issued 2013

A catalogue record for this publication is available from the British Library

ISBN 978-1-107-69039-4 Paperback

NOTE

LANCELOT ANDREWES [1555–1626], Bishop of Winchester, was famous during his life for his ability in controversy, his saintliness, and his learning. He has always had his importance for church historians, but by others he is remembered now for his *Devotions* and for his part in the making of the Authorised Version. A few critics, among them Canon Ottley and Mr T. S. Eliot, have admired the quality of his sermons. Andrewes' business here is exegesis. His interest lies only in the text and he does not consider his work finished until every word has directed a separate pencil of light into the heart of his subject. These sermons alone might seem to justify a belief in the verbal inspiration of the Bible. It is his theme which masters Andrewes. He carries his learning like a flower; it is no more to him than his quick humour and his witty experience of life. His friend Isaacson remembered him as "*stella prædicantium*...an Angell in the Pulpit," but he certainly spoke the language of men, even of common men. His style progresses with the imperturbable tattoo of a Morse signal. He escapes the muddiness of many of Donne's sermons and has no use for his ecstasies. Where everything is equally important there is no need for rhetoric.

The text followed is that of the first folio of 1629, its very few misprints being corrected —mostly on the evidence of later folios. In this reprint we have not been able to preserve at all points the spacing of the folio page, nor the copious and purposeful italicising of words other than Latin.

JOHN BUTT

GEOFFREY TILLOTSON

13 February 1932

A SERMON

Preached before the King's Majestie, at
Whitehall, on the XVI. of Aprill,
A.D. MDCIX. being EASTER DAY.

JOHN. Chap. XX. Ver. XIX.

*Cum ergo serò esset die illo, una Sabbatorum, et
fores essent clausæ, ubi erant Discipuli congregati propter metum Judæorum: venit Jesus, et
stetit in medio, & dixit eis, Pax Vobis.*

The same day then, at night, which was the
first day of the weeke, and when the doores
were shutt, where the Disciples were assembled for feare of the Jewes, came Jesus
and stood in the middest, and said to them,
Peace be unto you.

THIS is the first enter-view of Christ and His
Disciples: and this, His first speech, at His
first enter-view: Both, this day; the very first
day of His rising.

Five sundrie times, appeared He, this day.
[1]To Marie Magdalen: [2]To the Women comming from the Sepulcher: [3]To the two that
went to Emmaüs: [4]To Saint Peter:[5]And heere
now, to the Eleven and those that were with
them. The two first, to Women; the three
last to men: So, both Sexes. To Peter, and to
Mary Magdalen: So, to Sinners of both
Sexes. To the Eleven, as the Clergie; to
those with them, as the Laïtie: so to both
Estates. Abroad, at Emmaüs: at home,
heere. Betimes; and now, late. When they

Marginal notes:
[1]*Mar.* 16. 9.
[2]*Matt.* 28. 9.
[3]*Luc.* 24. 10.
[4]*Luc.* 24. 34.
[5]*In textu.*

were scattered, severally; and now jointly, when they were gathered togither. That no Sexe, Sort, Estate, Place or Time excepted:

Luc. 1. 78. but, as *Visitavit nos oriens ab alto*; so *Visitavit, occidens ab imò*: Rising from above, at His Birth; Rising, from beneath, at His Resurrection, He visited all.

But, of all the five, this is the chiefe. Those were, to one; as Peter: Or two; as those of Emmaüs: Or three, as the Women: This, to all: The more, the more Witnesses; the better for faith. Those, when they were scattered: this (heer) when they were all togither: The more togither, the more meet for this salutation heer, Peace be to you.

The Division.   Which Salutation is the very substance of
I.   the text: the rest but appendent, all.

In it, two things give forth themselves: 1. The Persons, to whom, *Vobis*. 2. The Matter of the Wish it selfe, Peace. The Persons are thus sett downe: *Discipuli, congregati, conclusi*: [1]His Disciples they were; [2]gathered; [3]and the doores shutt on them, for feare of the Jewes.

There will fall out besides, foure other points. [1]Christ His Site; that, He stood, when He wished it: [2]His Place; that, in the middst, He stood: [3]The Time; All this, the same day, the first day of the weeke, Sunday, Easter day: [4]and, the very time of the day; that, it was late.

II.   The speech, of it selfe, is a Salutation: any will so conceive it, at the first hearing.

And, if it were but so, and no more; that, were enough. Christ's salutations are not (as ours be) formall; but, good matter in them.

But, it is more then a Salutation, say the Fathers, for this reason. At meeting, men use to salute but once: within a verse, He repeateth it againe. So, it keeps not the law of a salutation: but, it is (certeinly) somwhat, besides. *Votum Christi*, they call it. *Votum pacis*, *votum Christi*: Christ's Vow, or wish: His Vow; and His first Vow.

Now, every Vow implieth an advise, at the least. What Christ wisheth to us, He wisheth us to. Every wish, so: But, if it be the wish of a Superior, in His Optative, there is an Imperative; His Wish, is a commaund, if he have witt that heares it. So that, these words (rightly understood) are both an Advise, and an Injunction to it; of the nature of an Edict. *Pax vobis*, is as much, as *Pacem habete in vobis*, Be at peace among *Mar.* 9. 50. your selves.

We are then, to joine with Christ; to follow Him, in His Wish. To whom He wisheth it: To all Christ's disciples, together, even to His whole Christian Church; and, even them, that (it may be) as little deserve it, as these heer did. [1]To make it *Caput voti*, our first Vow: yea, first & second; as Christ heere did. [2]*Oportet stantem optare*, to wish it, standing. [3]And, standing where Christ stood (that is materiall) in the midst.

⁴This day to do it; and thinke it pertinent to the time: It is *Votum Paschale*. As for *Serò*, we shall never need to take thought for it: It is never too soone; late enough, alwaies: if it be not too late; that, is all the feare.

❧❧❧ ❧❧❧ ❧❧❧ ❧❧❧ ❧❧❧ ❧❧❧ ❧❧❧

I.
The personall part of Christ's Salutation.
1.
Pax *and* vobis, *reconciled.*

The chiefe point, first: *Pax vobis*. The words are but two; yet, even between them, there seemeth to be no peace: but one (in a manner) opposite to the other. Looking to *Vobis* (the Persons) this should not be a salutation for them, *Pax*. Looking to the Salutation (Peace) it should not be, to those Persons; *Vobis*, to you. So that, our first worke will be, to make peace between the two words.

Vobis, to You. Will you know, who they be? To you, Peter, & John, and the rest. To

Matt. 26. 56.
72.
Mar. 14. 53.

you, of whom none stood by me: To you, of whom some ranne away, some denied, yea, forsware me. To you, of whom, all, every one shrunke away and forsooke me. How evill doth this greeting agree with this *Vobis*? Yet, even to these, *Venit, & stetit, & dixit*; He came, stood, and said, Peace be to you.

Mar. 14. 50.

Used by them, as He had been, no cause, He should come, or stand, or speake at all: Or, if speake, not thus. Not come to them, that went from Him: nor stand amongst them, that had not stood to Him: nor speake to them, that had renounced Him.

It is said, they feared the Jewes: All things *Joh.* 9. 22.
considered, they had more cause to feare
Him, and to looke for some reall revenge, at
His hands: If not that, some verball reproof;
a salutation, of another stile or tenour: And
well, if they might scape so. *Confitemini* *Psa.* 106. 1.
Domino, quia bonus; It is not so: No evill
deed, for all this: No, not so much as an
unkind word. Above that, they could looke
for; farr above that, they deserved, it is;
Pax vobis. You and I are at peace, you and I
are friends; Peace be unto you. This is His
first goodnesse: His making a peace between
Pax and *Vobis*.

This Speech to these Persons, is much Illo die, *that is*
mended, by adding the Time in the text; Primo die.
that, it was *illo die*; the day of His rising.
Pax Vobis, is a good speech, for Good-friday,
then, men grow charitable, when ready to
dye. But, on their Easter-day, at their rising,
the day when *Exaltavit Eum Deus*, the day of *Phil.* 2. 9.
their exaltation, they use to take other
manner spirits, and remember former
disgraces, with a farr other congie. *Hæc est
lex hominis*; Men doe thus: but, not Christ.
Neither their indignitie, *Vobis*; nor His own
dignitie changeth Him. Rising, exalted, the
very day of His exaltation, *illo die*, He saith,
Peace be unto you.

Another yet: That, it was *Primâ Sabbati*, Primâ Sabbati.
the very first day of the weeke: tooke no *Luc.* 24. 1.
long day for it: Nay, no day at all, but the
very first day. Joseph (exalted) dealt well

with his brethren; but, not the first day: it
was some time, first. He kept them in feare,
a while; but shewed himselfe, at the last.
Christ doth not so; hold them in suspense:
illo die, *primo die*, the same day, the first day,
He came, and shewed Himselfe, and sayd,
Peace be unto you.

Dixit.
not, respondit.

Yea, not so much as *dixit* (heer) but (as it
falls out) will beare a note. Even, that it is
dixit, and not *Respondit*; a Speech, not an
Answere. That He spake it, unspoken to:
He, to them, first; yer they, to Him. He might
well have stayed till then: and reason would,
they should first have sued for it. Yer they
aske it, He giveth it: and prevents them with
the blessing of peace. They first, in falling
out: He first, at making friends.

Psal. 21. 3.

A great comfort for poor sinners, when,
the many indignities, we have offered
Christ, shall present themselves before us, to
thinke of this *Vobis*. That, when the Disciples
had done the like, yet He forgatt all; and
spake thus kindly to them, this day: That He
will vouchsafe us the like (specially, if we
seeke it, He will) and say to us *Pax Vobis*.

Will ye remember now, to extend your
wish of Peace, ¹to them, that (it may be) deserve it as evill, as these, heer: Even, *his qui
longè*. ²To doe it, at our rising, at our high
day, when it is Easter with us: ³Not, to make
their hearts to pant, and eyes to faile first;
but, even *primâ Sabbati*, to doe it. ⁴And, not
to take state upon us, and be content, to

answer, Peace; and not speake: be moved for
it; but, not move it: yes, even move it,
first. If we do, we joine with Christ, in His
first part, the personall part of the wish.

Illis, and *illo die*, and *primo die*, what they *The persons to whom.*
were, we see; and in what sort. Yet, (not to
grate on this point altogither) some smoke yet
was there in the flaxe; some small remainders,
illices misericordiæ (as Tertullian) to move his
mercie: In these words, ¹*Discipuli*, ²*congregati*,
³*conclusi*, ⁴*propter timorem Judæorum*: That,
His Disciples (yet) they were; and, togither
they were; and, in feare of the Jewes, they
were shutt up.

Whatsoever, or howsoever they were els, *1. His Disciples.*
yet, they were His Disciples: Unprofitable *Luc. 17. 10.*
servants, yet Servants: Lost sonnes, yet *15. 24.*
Sonnes: forgetfull Disciples, yet Disciples.
His Disciples they were: and, howsoever
they had made a fault (as it seemeth) so
meant to hold themselves, still; and heer-
after to learne their lesson better.

And, I like well their feare: that, they *2. For, In feare of the Jewes.*
were afrayd of the Jewes. It shewes, there
were no good termes betwixt them; and that
they shutt their doores upon them, therefore
they meant not to go out to them, or seeke
Pax vobis of the Jewes. They had no meaning
(it seemeth) to give over Christ. If they had,
what need they feare the Jewes? The Jewes
would have done them no harme, they might
have sett open their doores, well enough.

And *Congregatis* (I take it) is no evill signe. *3. Assembled.*

2.

It would have been *Ex aliâ causâ*; for love,
rather then feare: And againe, for feare of
God, rather then of the Jewes. Yet, even
thus, I mis-like it not: And, much better this
feare, then that at the Passion: That,
scattered them one from another; every man
shift for one. This, makes them draw togither, and keepe togither, as if they meant
to stand out afresh. Which very [*Congregatis*]
makes them fitt for this Salutation. It
cannot well be sayd, *disgregatis*, to them that
are in sunder. *Unà*, is a disposition to
unitie; and gathering, to the binding up in
Mat. 23. 37.   the band of peace. Christ (that sayd, *Quoties
volui congregare!*) liked it well, to finde them
thus togither: And, His comming was, as to
take away their feare; so, to continue their
gathering, still.

And, shall we learne this, of the Disciples:
[1]If a fault fall out, not to give over schoole,
but to continue our Disciple-ship, still. [2]And,
not to goe over, to seeke our *Pax vobis*, at the
hands of His Enimies: To shutt out both
them, and their peace, too. [3]And lastly, not to
forsake the fellowship; to keepe togither, still.
For, being so togither, we are neerer our
Peace. This shall make Christ come and say
II.   it to us the sooner, and the more willingly.
The reall part.   The reall part, *Voti summa*, that which He
wisheth, is Peace. First, Why peace: Then,
I.   What peace.
Why Peace.   Why, Peace? Is there nothing more worth
the wishing? Nothing more, of it selfe;

Nothing more fit for these persons, this place, and this time.

Of it selfe: *Votum pacis, Summa votorum.* It is, all wishes, in one; Nothing more to be wished. For, *in brevi voce Breviarium*, this little word is a Breviarie of all, that good is.

To shew how, a little: *quàm bonum*, how good, how worth the wishing it is. It is *tam bonum*, so good, as, without it, nothing is good. With it (saith Salomon) an hand-full of herbes; without it, an hous-full of sacrifices, is not good. With trouble and vexation, nothing is good; nothing is to be wished. *1. As, good.* *Psal. 133. 1.* *Pro. 15. 16. 17.* *Pro. 17. 1.*

And as, without it, nothing is to be wished: so, all that is to be wished (all good) is within it. *Evangelizantium pacem, evangelizantium bona; quia, in pace, omnia bona*: To bring newes of peace, is, to bring newes of all good things; for, all good things are, in peace. *Bona*, is the true glosse or exposition of peace. *Rom. 10. 15.*

Quàm bonum, you know: And, *quàm jucundum*, too: Both good and pleasant; and pleasant, not onely, as Aarons ointment (which was, onely pleasant:) but, as Hermon dew, which brings profit with it. *Abundantia pacis* (saith the Psalme) Peace, and Plentie goe togither. *2. Pleasant.* *Psal. 133. 1.* *3. Profitable.* *Psal. 72. 7.*

And yet, how much it is to be wished, this sheweth, *Pacem te poscimus omnes*: All wish it: Angells wish it (Heaven, to Earth) *Pax in terris*: And Men wish it (Earth, to Heaven) *Pax in cœlis.* God wisheth it: most kindly for Him; *Deus pacis, pacem Dei*; the God of *4. Wished by all.* *Luc. 2. 14.* *2. Cor. 13. 11.*

Phil. 4. 7.

peace, the peace of God. Yea, the enemie of all peace wisheth it: for, he complaines,

Luc. 4. 34.

Venisti nos inquietare, are ye come to trouble us? So, he would not be troubled, that troubles all; but, sett all togither by the eares, and sitt quiet himselfe.

But, it is much for the honor of peace, that, *cum bellum geritur, pax quæritur*: Even militar persons, with sword in one hand and fire in the other give this for their Embleme, *Sic quærimus pacem*, Thus with sword and fire, seeke we peace. As, seeke it, at last, they must; we must, all. Best, *primâ Sabbati*: but, *Serò*, sooner or later, come to it we must: If it be not the first, it must be our last.

And by Christ often

But, if there were nothing els, this onely were enough; and, though there be many, this chiefly doth shew it: That our Saviour Christ, so often, so diverse waies, so earnestly

Joh. 14. 27.

wisheth it. Going, He did it, *Pacem meam do vobis*: And now comming, He doth it.

Joh. 16. 33.

Sitting, He did it (Chap. 16.) and now,

Luk. 2. 14.

standing. Living, when He was borne, *Pax in terris*, *Xenium Christi*, It was Christ's

Chap. 14. 27.

New-yeares-gift: Dying, when He was to suffer, *Pacem meam relinquo vobis*, it was *Legatum Christi*, Christ's Legacie. And now (heere) rising againe, it is His wish, still. To shew, not only the good of this life, but of the

Chap. 17. 21.

next, to be in peace. Prayed for it (Chap. 17.)

Luk. 19. 42.

Payed for it (Chap. 18.) Wept for it; O if thou hadst knowen the things that pertaine to thy peace! Wept for it; and bledd for it:

therefore, immediately (the very next words)
He sheweth them His hands and His side:
As much to say; See, what I have suffered,
to procure your peace: Your peace cost me
this: *Pax vobis* cost *Crux mihi*; See, you hold
it deere. Now (sure) if there were any one
thing better then other, those hands would
not have with-held it, and that heart would
wish it. And, Peace it doth wish: therefore,
nothing more to be wished. Complete it is,
Votum pacis, Summa votorum.

There need no other signe be given, but *Jon.* 1. 12.
that, of the Prophet Jonas; that Christ
wished his wish: So the tempest may cease,
and peace (as a calme) ensue, spare me not;
take me, cast me into the Sea; make me a
Peace-offering, and kill me. This, is enough
to shew, it is to be wished; to make it
pretious in our eyes. For, we under-value it,
at too low a rate, when (that, which cost so
deere) for every trifling ceremonie, we are
ready to lose it. Our faint perswasion in this
point, is the cause, we are faint in all the rest.

Well, though this be thus good; yet good it
selfe is not good, unlesse it be in season,
come fitly. Doth this so? Every way fitly
[1] For the Persons: [2] For the Place: [3] and for the
Time.   1.

The Persons: both [1] Christ by whom; and *And now, fitly*
[2] they, to whom it is wished. 1. Christ, by *for the Persons.*
[1]By whom;
whom: *Decet Largitorem pacis hæc salutatio* *Christ.*
(saith Cyrill) It is meet, for Him, to give
peace, that made peace: Nay, *Ipse est Pax* *Ephes.* 2. 14.

nostra (saith the Apostle;) and, for Peace, what fitter salutation, then Peace?

² *To whom:*
The Disciples.

2. They, to whom: for, they needed it: with God, they had no peace, whom they had provoked: Nor peace with men; not with the Jewes about them: Nor peace with themselves, for they were in feare, and night-feare, which is the worst of all others. Fit for them; and they, for it: for, together they were, and so, not unfit to entertaine it.

2.
For the Place.

And, with the Place, it suiteth well. For, they were shut up, as men environed and beleaguered with their enemies: *Conclusi, & derelicti*, shut up and forsaken: And to such, Peace is ever welcome.

3.
For the Time.

And, for the time, seasonable. For, after a falling out, Peace is so: And, after a victorie, Peace is so. Fitt therefore, for this day, the day of the Resurrection: for, till then, it was not in kind. The great battaile was not fought: The last enemie (death) was not overcome. Never, till now: but, now the last enemie is conquered, now it is in season.

1. Cor. 15. 26.

4.
For the thing it-
selfe:
Peace, a resur-
rection.

And, for the thing it selfe, Peace, is a kind of Resurrection. When Christ was risen, His Disciples were dead. Those dead affections of sorrow and feare, when they seise throughly upon men, what are they, but *Mors ante mortem*? Upon good newes of Joseph, Jacob is said to revive: as if, before, he had beene given for dead. It was their case, heere. The house was to them, as their grave; and the doore as the grave-stone; and they buried

Gen. 45. 27.

in feare: when they saw Him, in the next verse, and were thus saluted by Him, they gatt hope, were glad (that is) revived againe. For, if those were the pangs of death, peace (after a sort) is a resurrection: and so, a fit wish for the time.

And, to say truth, Peace is never kindly, till *Never kindly till* then. They define felicitie shortly, to be *then.* nothing els but *Pax desiderij*. For, give the desire perfect peace, and no more needs, to make us happy. Desire hath no rest; and will let us have none, till it have what it would; and, till the Resurrection, that will not be.

1. *Pax & pressura*, our Saviour opposeth (Chap. 16.) If we be pinched with any want, *Chap. 16. 33.* Desire hath no peace. 2. Let us want nothing (if it were possible) No peace, yet: *Pax & Scandalum* (the Psalmist opposeth:) When *Psal. 119. 165.* we have what we would, somewhat commeth to us, we would not; somewhat thwarts us: Till *non est eis scandalum*, till that be had away, desire hath no peace. 3. Let that be had away, yet a new warre there commeth. Peace and feare, are (heere) opposed. We are well: neither *pressura*, nor *Scandalum*: but, we feare *tolletur a vobis*, that it will not hold, or we shall not hold. The last enemie will not let us be quiet. Till he be overcome, our desire hath no perfect peace. That, will not be, till the Resurrection. But, then, it is *Pax plena, pura, perpetua*: full without want; pure, without mixture of offensive matter;

and *perpetuall*, without all feare of forgoing, of *tolletur a vobis*. And that, is *pax desiderij*; and that, is perfect felicitie: The state of the Resurrection; and the wish of the Resurrection day.

2.
What Peace?

Thus (we see) good it is: and, fit it is. It remaines, we see, What it is; What, peace. When we speake of Peace, the nature of the word leadeth us, to aske, With whom? And they be diverse. But, as diverse as they be, it must be understood of all; though, of some-one, more especially then the rest.

[1] *Peace with God*

There is a peace above us in heaven, with God: that, first. They were wrong, heere: their feare ran all upon the Jewes: It should have looked higher. The Jewes they kept out, with shutting their doores: Against God, no doore can be shut. First, peace with Him: and, with Him, they have peace, to whom Christ saith *Pax vobis*.

[2] *With our owne hearts.*

There is another peace, within us, *in sinu*, with our heart. For, betweene our spirit and our flesh, there is in manner of a Warre: The lusts of the flesh, even Militant, wage Warre 1. *Pet.* 2. 11. (saith Saint Peter) against the soule: And, where there is a warre, there is a peace, too. This is peace with feare, heere. Which warre is sometime so fearefull, as men, to ridd themselves of it, ridd themselves of life and all; Conclude a peace there. This, followeth of the first: If all be well above, all is well within.

With all men.

There is a peace without us, in earth, with

men, with all men: The Apostle warrants it;
peace with the Jewes heere and all. I will
never feare, to make civill peace, a part of
Christ's wish; nor, of his *Beati Pacifici*, *Matt. 5. 9.*
neither. He will be no worse at Easter, then
at Christ-masse, He was: at this, His second;
then, at that his first birth. Then, *Janus* was
shut, and peace over all the world. *Orbem* *Tertullian.*
pacatum was ever a clause in the prayers of *Apolog.*
the Primitive Church; that the World might
be quiet.

Yet is not this the peace of Christ's *¹Among them-*
principall entendment; but, their peace, to *selves.*
whom Christ spake: *Pax Discipulorum; Pax*
vobis, inter vos: Peace among them, or
betweene themselves. It was the ointment on *Psal. 133. 2.*
Aaron's head: Aaron, that had the care of the
Church. It was the dew that fell upon Sion:
Sion, the place, where the Temple stood.
The peace of Jerusalem; that it may be once, *Psal. 122. 3.*
as a citie at unitie within it selfe. The
primitive peace; that the multitude of *Act. 4. 32.*
Beleevers may be of one heart and one minde.
All the rest depend upon our peace with
God; and, our peace with Him, upon this:
ᵃ*Pacem habete inter vos*, and *Deus pacis erit* *ᵃMarke 9. 50.*
Phi. 4. 9.
vobiscum. The peace of Jerusalem; ᵇthey shall *ᵇPsa. 122. 6.*
prosper that love it, (saith David.) ᶜJoy shall *ᶜPro. 12. 20.*
be to them that counseile it (saith Salomon.)
ᵈBlessed shall they be, that make it (saith *ᵈMatt. 5. 9.*
Christ.) How great a reward should he finde
in heaven; how glorious a name should he
leave on earth, that could bring this to passe!

¹*Peace, Christ's wish.*

This, is Christ's wish: And, what is become of it? If we looke upon the Christian world, we see it not; it is gone, as if Christ had never wished it. Betweene Jehu and Jeroboam, Salomon's seed went to wracke. Jehu, his proceedings (like his chariot wheeles) headlong and violent. But Jehu is but a brunt; too violent, to last long. Jeroboam is more dangerous: who makes it his wisedome, to keepe up a Schisme in Religion; they shall sway both parts more easily. God forbid, we should ever thinke Jeroboam wiser then Salomon. If peace were not a wise thing, the Wisest man's name should not have beene Salomon. A greater then Salomon would never have said, *Habete salem & Pacem*; If you have any salt, you will have peace. Sure, when the Disciples lost their peace, they lost their wisedome: Their wisedome, and their strength both. They were stronger, by *congregatis*, then by *clausis foribus*; more safe, by their being together, then any door could make them.

Matt. 12. 42.

Mar. 9. 50.

It is, as Christ told us (Luk. 10. where, He prescribes this forme of salutation) it speeds, or it misses, thereafter, as it meets with the Sonne of peace: Speeds, if it finde him; if not, comes backe againe, and takes no place.

Luk. 10. 5. 6.

Well, though it doe not, we must still hold us to Christ's Wish: and, when all failes, still there must be *Votum pacis in corde*; though enmitie in the act, yet peace in the heart still.

Still, it must hold, *Amicus, ut non alter*; *Inimicus, ut non idem*: friends, as if never otherwise; Enemies, as if not ever so. *Quasi torrens, bellum*: warre, like a land-flood, that will be drie againe: *Quasi fluvius, pax*; Peace, as a river, never drie, but to runne stil and ever.

But yet, many times we aske, and have not, *Jam. 4. 3.* because we aske not aright (saith Saint James:) We know not the things, that belong to our Peace; we erre in the order, manner, site, place, or time.

1.

The Order: which helpeth much, first it *The order of it:* is; first, *Primum & ante omnia; Caput fidei*; *first wished.* the prime of His wishes. No sooner borne, but *Pax in terris*: No sooner risen, but *Pax vobis: Apertio labiorum*, the very opening of his lipps was, with these words: The first words: at the first meeting: On the very first day. It is a signe, it is so in His heart. That, which most greeveth us, we first complaine of: and, that which most affecteth us, ever soonest speake of. This, is the first error. That which was first with Christ, is last with Christians: and, I would it were so (last:) for, then, it were some: Now, scarce any at all, as it seemeth.

2.

In the Manner: for, first is but first, that is *The Manner:* but once. This, is first, and second. Heere, *thrise wished.* He saith it: and, within a verse, He is at it againe. Nay, first, second, and third: [1]in this, [2]the XXI, and [3]XXVI. verses: As if (like *Actio*, in Rhetorique) all in all.

All Christ's vowes are to be esteemed; specially, His solemne vowes: And His speeches; chiefly, those He goeth over and over againe. That which, by Him, is double and treble said, would not, by us, be singly regarded. He would have it better marked: therefore He speaketh it the second time. He would have it yet sinke deeper; therefore, the third also. We fault, in the manner. Once, we doe it (it may be:) but, upon any repulse, we give over: if it come not at first, we go not to it *Secundò & tertiò, repetitis vicibus*. We must not leave at once, that Christ did so oft.

3.
His Site in wishing it.
Stetit.

The second error is; we aske it, sitting (I feare;) and Christ stood: His standing imports something. Standing, is the site of them, that are ready to goe about a matter: as

Exod. 12. 11.

they, to take their journey, in the XII. of Exodus. That Site, is the Site of them, that wish for peace: *Oportet stantem optare*. A Sedentarie desire (it may be) we have; but, loth to leave our cushion: We would, it were well; but, not willing, to disease our selves. *Utinam hoc esset laborare*, said he, that lay along and stretched himselfe. So say we: Peace we would; but, standing is painfull. Our wish hath lipps, but no leggs.

Esay. 52. 7.
Rom. 10. 15.

But, it could not be said: Beautifull are the feete of them that bring Peace, if the feet had nothing to do, in this businesse. With sitting and wishing, it will not be had.

Psal. 34. 14.

*Peace will hide it selfe; it must be sought

out: It will fly away, it must be pursued.
This then, is a point, wherein, we are to conforme our selves to Christ: as well to use our
leggs, as to open our lipps for it. To stand,
is *Situs voventis*: To hold up the hands,
Habitus orantis. The meaning of which
ceremonie, of lifting up the hands with
prayer, is, *Ut, pro quo quis oret, pro eo laboret*,
what we pray for, we should labour for:
what we wish for, stand for. We see, Christ
sheweth His hands and His feet; to shew,
what must be done with both, for it. If we
should be put to doe the like, I doubt, our
wish hath never a good legg, to stand on.

4.

To stand then: But, to stand, in a certain *His Place:*
place. Every where to stand, will not serve *In medio.*
the turne. *Stetit in medio*, that standing place
is assigned for it, thus guiding our feet into *Luc.* 1. 79.
the way of Peace. And, the Place, is materiall,
for peace. All bodies naturall never leave
moving, are never quiet, till they recover their
proper places; and, there, they find peace.
The midst is Christ's place, by Nature. He, *By nature.*
is the second person *in divinis*; and so, the
middle-most of the other two. And, on
earth, follow Him (if you will) you shall not
(lightly) find Him out of it: Not, according to
the letter, speaking of the materiall place.
At His birth; *In medio animalium*, in the *Luc.* 2. 7.
Stable. After (a child) *In medio Doctorum*, in 46.
the Temple. After (a man) *Medius vestrûm*
stetit (saith John Baptist) in the midst of the *Joh.* 1. 26.
people; saith He of Himselfe, *Ecce Ego in*

Luc. 22. 27.   *medio vestri*, in the midst of His Apostles. At
23. 33.   His death, it fell to His turne likewise, that
place; even then, He was in the midst. And
now (rising) there He is (we see). They, in
the midst of the Jewes: and He, in the
midst of them. After this, in Patmos, Saint
Apoc. 7. 17.   John saw Him in heaven, in the middst of the
1. 13.   throne: in earth, walking in the middst of the
Candlesticks.   And, at the last day, He
Matth. 25. 33.   shalbe in the midst, too, of the sheepe on His
right hand, and the goates on His left. All
which shew, the place and He, sort very well.

By office, as a   But, were it not naturall for Him, as the
Mediator.   case standeth, there, He is to stand, being to
give peace. No place so fitt, for that purpose:
None, so kindly, as it. His Office being, to be
1. *Tim.* 2. 5.   a Mediator, *Medius* between God and man,
where should a Mediator stand, but *in
Medio?*

The reason of it.   Besides, the two qualities of good, being to
be *Diffusivum* and *Unitivum*; that, is the
fittest place, for both. To distribute; best
done, from the center. To unite, likewise;
soonest meet, there. The place it selfe hath a
vertue specially to unite: which is never done
but by some middle thing. If we will conclude, we must have a *Medius terminus*: Els,
we shall never gett *Majus* and *Minus ex-
tremum* to come togither. Nor, in things
naturall; either combine two elements dis-
agreeing in both qualities, without a middle
symbolizing with both: Nor flesh and bone,
without a cartilage between both. As for

things morall; there, the middle is all in all.
No vertue without it. In Justice; encline the
ballance, one way or other, the even peize is
lost: *Et, opus Justitiæ, pax*: Peace is the very
worke of Justice. And the way, to peace, is
the mid way: neither to the right hand, too
much; nor, to the left hand, too little. In a
word; all analogie, symmetrie, harmonie, in
the world, goeth by it.

It commeth all to this: The manner of the
Place doth teach us, what manner of Affec-
tion is to be in them, that wish for, or stand
for peace. The place is indifferent, æqually
distant, alike neer, to all. There, pitch the
Arke; that, is the place for it. Indifferencie
in carriage, preserveth peace: By forgoing
that, and leaning to extremities, it is lost.
Thither we must get againe, and there stand,
if ever we shall recover it. *Discessit a medio*
lost it: *Stetit in medio* must restore it.

Therefore when you heare men talke of
peace, marke whither they stand where they
should. If with the Pharisee, to the corners,
either by partialitie one way, or prejudice,
another; no good will be done. When God
will have it brought to passe, such minds He
will give unto men; and make them meet, to
wish it, seeke it, and find it.

A little (now) of the time. This, was ⁵·
Christ's wish, at this time: And Christ *The Time:
In illo die.*
never speakes out of season. Therefore, a
speciall interest hath this Feast, in it. It is
Votum Paschale, and this is *Festum pacis*.

1. Cor. 11. 16. And sure, *Habemus talem consuetudinem,*
& Ecclesiæ Dei: Such a custome we have,
and so, the Church of God hath used it; to
take these words of Christ, in the nature of
an Edict for pacification, ever at this time.
That, whatsoever become of it, all the yeare
beside, this time should be kept a time of
peace; we should seeke it, and offer it: seeke
it, of God; and offer it, each to other.

There hath not, these sixteen hundred
yeares, this day passed, without a Peace-
offering. And, the Law of a Peace-offering
is; he, that offers it, must take his part of it;
eat of it, or it doth him no good. This day
therefore, the Church never failes, but setts
forth her Peace-offering: the Body, whose
hands were heer shewed; and, the Side,
Col. 1. 20. whence issued *Sanguis crucis*, the blood that
pacifieth all things in earth & heaven: that
we, in and by it, may this day, renew the
Covenant of our peace. Then can it not be,
but a great grief, to a Christian heart, to see
many, this day, give Christ's peace the
hearing, and, there is all; heare it, and then
turne their backs on it; every man go his
way, and forsake his peace: instead of
seeking it, shunn it; and, of pursuing, turne
away from it.

phe. 4. 20. We have not so learned Christ: Saint Paul
hath not so taught us. His Rule it is: Is
1. Cor. 5. 7. Christ our Passover offered for us (as, now,
8. He was?) *Epulemur itaque* (That, is his
Conclusion) Let us then keep a Feast, a

Feast of sweet bread, without any sowre
levin, that is, of Peace without any malice.

So to doe: and, even then (this day) when
we have the peace-offering in our hands,
then, to remember, and alwaies (but then,
specially) to joine with Christ, in His wish;
to put into our hearts, and the hearts of all,
that professe His name (theirs specially, that
are of all others most likely to effect it) that
Christ may have His wish, and there may be
peace through the Christian world: That we
may once all partake togither, of one peace-
offering; and with one mouth, and one mind,
glorifie God, the Father of our Lord Jesus
Christ.

A SERMON

Preached before the King's Majesty, in
the Cathedral Church at Durham, on
the XX. of Aprill, A.D. MDCXVII, being
EASTER DAY.

MATTH. Chap. XII. Ver. XXXIX. Ver. XL.

Qui respondens ait illis: Generatio &c.

But He answered and said unto them; An evill
and adulterous generation seeketh a signe, but
no signe shalbe given unto it, save the signe
of the Prophet Jonas.
For, as Jonas was three daies and three nights,
in the Whale's belly; so shall the Sonne of
man be, three daies and three nights, in the
heart of the earth.

THE Signe of the Prophet Jonas, is the signe
of the Resurrection: And, this is the Feast of
the Resurrection. Being then the Signe of
this Feast, at this Feast to be set up: *Signum
Temporis, in Tempore Signi*, The Signe of the
time, at the time of the signe, most properly,
ever.

The Summe.   The words are an answere, of Christ's (in
this verse) to a motion, of the Pharisees (in
the last) They would see a Signe. The
answere is negative, but qualified. There is in
it, a *Non*, and a *Nisi*: *Non dabitur*, none
shalbe given them. Indeed none should:
They were worthy of none. Yet saith He not,
Non simply. His *Non*, is with a *Nisi*, *Non*

dabitur, nisi; it is with a limitation, with a but:
None, but, that. So, that: So, one shalbe. In
the *Non*, is their desert: in the *Nisi*, His
goodnesse: that, though they were worthy
none, yet gives them one, though.

Gives them one: and one, that is worth the
giving. Put *Non* and *Nisi* togither, it is a
Non nisi. If you speake of a Signe, None to it:
a Signe, *instar omnium*.

This Signe, is the Signe of the Prophet
Jonas. Of him, diverse other waies, and
namely this: That as he was in the Whale's
belly, so was Christ in the heart of the earth.
There they were, either.

And, that which makes up the Signe,
Three daies apeece: Three daies, and no
longer.

And then, as Jonas cast up by the Whale;
so Christ rose againe from the dead; and
both, the third day. So that, upon the matter,
the Substance of this Signe, is Christ's
resurrection; and the Circumstance of it, is
this very day.

We will divide it no otherwise, then already *The Division.*
we have: [1]into the *Non*, *Non dabitur*: [2]the
Nisi, *Non dabitur nisi*: [3]& the *Non nisi*,
Non nisi Signum Jonæ.

The *Non*, the deniall first: *Non dabitur eis*.   I.
And the reason is, in *Eis*, in the parties. For,
they [1]an evill, and [2]adulterous, and a [3]genera-
tion of such (three brands sett upon them:)
Eis, to them, to such as them, no Signe to be
given: none at all.

II. Then the *Nisi*: *Non dabitur, Nisi*. For,
though they were such, as little deserved any,
yet Christ, of His goodnesse, will not cast
them quite of. None He will give, but. So,
one He will give: A Signe they shall have.

III. And that, no triviall, or petie Signe (to
give it His due) but, in very deed, a *Signum,
non nisi; Non nisi Signum Jonæ*, that is,
insigne Signum, a Signe signall: marke them
all, None like it.

And that is, the Signe of the Prophet
Jonas, comming forth of the Whale's jawes,
half out and half in. In which Signe, there
are (upon the point) three *Sicuts*.

1. The Parties first; as Jonas, so the Sonne
of man (that is) himselfe.

2. Wherein, the Place. That as the one was
in the Whales bellie; so was the other in the
bowels of the earth.

3. Last, in time. Either, three daies and three
nights just, and but three daies, and then
forth againe. There they were, and there
(both) the same time: the Places diverse;
the time, the same.

So, Jonas, the Signe of Christ: and the
Whale's bellie, the signe of Christ's grave.
Jona's three daies, the Signe of Christ's three
daies, [1] Goodfriday, [2] Yesterday, [3] and to day.

Which three daies, when we shall come to
calculate them, they will give us three stands,
and make (as it were) three Signes in one;
each day, his severall Signe.

The letter of the Text saith, there they

were: [1]we are caried then, to aske, how came
they thither. The text saith, there they were,
but three daies: [2]We are caried then to aske,
how came they thence.

[1]Jona's state before he came into the Whale:
[2]His state while there: [3]His state getting
thence.

Conforme in Christ. [1]Goodfriday, when,
as Jonas went downe the Whale's throat, so
Christ layd in His grave: [2]Easter eve, while
there He lay: [3]And this (which is now the
third day) when, as Jonas cast up on drie
land; So Christ risen from death, to the life
immortall.

So have you (as in a signe) set forth
[1]Christ's death, by Jona's drowning: [2]Christ's
buriall, by Jona's abode there: [3]Christ's
resurrection, by Jona's emersion again.

As *Christus sepultus*, by Jonas *absorptus*:
So *Christus resurgens*, by Jonas *emergens*.
[1]Jonas going downe the Whale's throat, of
Christ put into His sepulcher: [2]Jona's
appearing againe, out of the Whale's mouth,
of Christ's arising out of His Sepulcher. All,
in Jonas, shadowed: And, in Christ, fullfilled.

In these three daies, these three Signes:
And, in them, three Keyes of our faith,
three Articles of our Creed, [1]*Mortuus*,
[2]*Sepultus*, [3]and *Resurrexit*, [1]Christ's death,
[2]buriall, and [3]rising again.

And last, what this Signe portends, or *Psal.* 86. 17.
signifies. That, whatsoever it was, to them;
to us, it is *Signum in bonum*, a Signe boding

good to-us-ward: A signe of favour and good hope, which we have by the resurrection of our Saviour. Specially, if we have the true Signature of it, which is true repentance.

I.
The deniall of a Signe: Non dabitur.

Jud. 6. 36.

2. *King.* 20. 8.

To aske a Signe, is (of it selfe) not evill; Good men, holy Saints have done it. Gedeon asked one of God and had it: He is painted with the fleece (that is, the Signe given him) in his hand. Ezechias asked one and had it too: In the Sundiall of Ahaz, the shadow went ten degrees backe. Yet, this suit heer is denied by Christ: And Christ denieth nothing that is good: Specially, not with hard termes as heer (we see) He doth.

The reason, in Eis, *the men.*

Somewhat is amisse sure: and it is not in the Signe, or in the suite, but in *Eis*, the men: the suit was not evill, the Suitours were. In three words, three brands sett upon them: [1]Evill, [2]adulterous, [3] a generation of evill and adulterous.

They were Evill.

1. Evill. There be markes of evill minded men, even in their very suit. They would see a Signe: If they had never seen any before, it had not beene evill: but, they came now,

Vers. 22.

from a Signe; they had scarse wiped their eyes, since they saw one (the Signe of the blind and dumbe man, made to see and speake) immediately before: It was *Spirans adhuc*, yet warme, as they say. That, they saw; and saw they not a Signe? A little

before, even in this very Chapter, a withered *Vers. 10.*
hand was restored to another: What, could
not they see a Signe, in that, neither? Goe
backe to the Chapters before, ye shall have
no lesse then a dozen signes, one after
another: and, come they now with a *Volumus* *Vers. 38.*
videre? They would have that shewed them,
that, when it is shewed, they will not see: A
bad minde this, certeinly.

2. Nay worse yet: For ye shall note malice in *Nay maliciously*
them (which is the worst kinde of evill.) For, *evill.*
if ye marke, this *Volumus* of theirs, is, with a
kinde of spite, with a kinde of disgrace, to
those he had shewed before. They would
see one: as who should say; those were none,
they had seene: that was none they saw, even
now. Maliciously: If He shewed none, then
He was no-bodie; could not indeed shew
any; and so vilifie Him with the people: If
He shewed one, then carp and cavill at it,
as they did at that even now: Say, it was done
by the black art. So, cavill out one; and call
for another, to deprave that too.

3. Nay (which is worst of all) Evill and *And absurdly*
absurd men (saith the Apostle.) When is *evill.*
that? *Vidi iniquitatem & contradictionem,* *2. Tim. 3. 13.*
saith the Psalmist. Ye shall see, how ab- *Psal. 55. 9.*
surdly they contradict themselves. But even
now, they charged Him, to worke by the
devill: and heer now, they come, and would
have Him shew a miracle. The devill cannot
shew a miracle; a tricke of *Sorcerie* he can:
Such may be done by the claw of the devill:

miracles not, but by the finger of God, by power divine. Him then, Him, whom they even now had pronounced, to deale with the devill; Him come they to now, for a miracle. So absurdly malicious, as they cared not, in their malice, to contradict themselves. To men, so evill, so maliciously evill, so absurdly evill, *Signum non dabitur eis*.

Well: howsoever they might erre that way, the men otherwise to be respected, they were so vertuous men, so streight livers. See ye not their phylacteries, how broad they weare them? Nor that neither (saith Christ;) but, evill, and adulterous too. As, of evill minds, so of evill lives, too. Ye shall come now, to the uncasing of a Pharisee. For, Christ lifts up their phylacteries, and shewes what lurkes under them.

For, by adulterous, I understand not, as if He charged them, they were borne of adulterie, came into the world the wrong way: the seed of Canaan, and not of Juda: As, having nothing in them of the Patriarchs; So nothing lesse, then their children, of whom they bare themselves so much. This, is *adulterina* rather, then *adultera*: children of the adulterers, rather then adulterous themselves. And, that was no fault of theirs: And Christ upbraideth no man, but with his owne faults.

Nor, I understand it not, of spirituall adulterie; though, that way, they might be charged, as leaving Him the true Spouse, the

true Messias; taking no notice of Him, passing
by Him, went after such as had adulterate
the truth of God, by devises of their owne
taking up: Not with Idolatrie (perhapps) but
(which is as evill, and differs but a letter)
with idiolatrie: For, to worship images, and
to worshipp men's own imaginations, comes
all to one. That, they were faulty of: (and I
pray God we be free.) But this, is mysticall
adulterie, and I would make, as no more
miracles, so no more mysteries, then needs
I must.

For my part, I see no harme, to take the
word in the native sense, without figure, for
men given to commit that sin, the sin of
adulterie. For (for all their deepe fringes)
all was not well that way: as is plaine, by
John VIII. Where, not one of them durst *Joh.* 8. 1.
take up a stone, to cast at the woman taken in
adulterie: but slunck away one after another,
till there was not one left. Christ toucheth
upon that string: to shew, what heavenly
men these were, that would have a signe from
heaven, and none els serve them. Were not
these meet men, to sue for a signe? Were not
a signe even cast away upon them?

But, this is not all. For, this they were *A generation of*
(saith our Saviour) not heer and there a man *such.*
of them; but the whole bunch was no better:
not the persons onely, but the Generation so:
not a good, of them all. And such, you shall
observe, there be: Not onely, such men, but
such Generations of men, and faults (suppose

of lying, swearing, and such like) rooted in a
stocke; kept even *in traduce* (as it were) and
derived downe *ab avis atavisque*, from the
father to the sonne, by many descents, in a
kinde of hereditarie propagation.

Salomon in his time noted foure of them:
[1]One, a generation unkind to their parents,
and their children, so to them for it: [2]Another,
pure in their owne eyes: [3]A third of high
eyebrowes: [4]A fourth, cruel hearted, whose
teeth were as knives to shred the poor of the
earth, shred them small.

Pro. 30. 11.
12.
13.
14.

Such were these: and adulterie made way
for such. For, *ubi corrupta sunt semina*, where
a generall corruption that way, no good to be
hoped for; the Countrie will not last long.
By this, Christ had said enough; and shewed,
that *non dabitur eis*, is a fit answer for these.

Now, this ye shall marke; the worse the
men, the more importune ever, and the
harder to satisfie. They must have signes,
and signes upon signes, and nothing will
serve them: As, no lesse then foure severall
times were they at Christ. [1]Heer: [2]in the
XVI. Chapter: [3]Mar. VIII. [4]Luc. XI. And
still to see a signe. As oft as they came, this
had been their right answere: to dispatch
them, with a *Non dabitur*, and no more adoe.
Other answere let them have none: Even
absolutely none at all: For, none they should
have had.

Chap. 16. 4.
Mar. 8. 11.
Luc. 11. 29.

II.
*The deniall
qualified* Non,
Nisi.

Yet saith He not, None they shall have.
He wilbe better to them, then they deserve:

Christ wilbe Christ: *Redit ad ingenium*:
Forgetts now all, He had said erewhile. And,
an evill and an adulterous generation though
they be, yet a signe they shall have, for all
that. Not simply None then, but *Non nisi*,
None save; the Negative is qualified: so
qualified, as upon the matter it proves an
Affirmative. The *Nisi* destroyes the *Non*:
Non dabitur nisi (that is) *dabitur*. So, one
they shall have: Though not now presently,
at their *volumus*, at their whistling (as it
were) but after, when He saw the time: And,
though (perhapps) not such a one, as they
would have phansied, yet such a one, as they
rather need, and would doe them more good:
(that is) one for their want, not for their
wanton desires.

And that is the reason, why none but it:
For, no Signe needed, but it. For, without
others, well they might be; without this,
they or we, could not well be. For, *oportuit
Christum pati*; It behooved Christ, Christ *Luc. 24. 26.*
ought to dye and rise againe.

None but that? Why afterward, between
this and His passion, He shewed diverse
others: and how then saith He, none but it?
Signes (indeed) He shewed: yet, not any of
them so pregnant for the purpose, they
sought, as was this. They sought a Signe of
the season, as by the XVI. Chapter is plaine: *Chap. 16. 4.*
that this was the time, the Messias was to
come. To put them out of doubt of that; to
that point, none so forcible, as His death and

rising againe, figured in that of Jonas. That,
and none but that. All He did els, the
Prophetts had done the like: Given Signes
from heaven (which they heer sought;) yea
even raised the dead. But raise Himselfe
being dead, get forth of the heart of the
earth, when once he was in; that passed their
skill: Never a Patriarch or Prophet of them
all, could doe that: *Non Nisi*, None but He.
So as, therein He shewed Himselfe indeed,
to be the true and undoubted Messias, and
never so els, in any signe of them all.

For, Signes being compounded of Power
and Goodnesse (not Power alone, but
Power and Goodnesse, that is, the benefit or
good of them, they be done for:) Never so
generall, so universall, so great a Good, as by
Christ's death (as it might be Jona's casting
in:) Nor ever so great, so incomparably
great a Power, as by raising Himselfe from
death to life (set forth in Jona's casting up
againe:) Those twaine, by these twaine,
more manifest, then by any other. The Signe
of the greatest Love and power (Love, to die;
power, to rise) that ever was wrought.

III.
This Signe
Signum non
nisi
*a signe para-
mount.*

This *Nisi* then, is a *Non nisi* in a new sense:
A None such, a Signe paramount. All els
nothing in comparison of it. I keepe you too
long from it.

The Signe is laid in the Prophet Jonas,
Sicut Jonas: and we are much bound to God,
for laying it in him: they, and we both. And
Jonas is a *Non nisi*: such a Signe, for us, and

(besides) so many peculiars of Christ, in him,
as (in effect) no signe but he.

First, for them, for an evill and adulterous *For them*, Pro-
generation, no signe so meete to be given as pheta peccator.
he. For, Jonas, and *non nisi Jonas*, was
Propheta peccator, the trespasser or Sinning
Prophet, among them all. Sinners (I know)
they were all: they confesse as much themselves: But, for transgressing the expresse
Commaundement of God, in not obeying
God's immediate call; therein, none of the
rest to be tainted: He onely was *Propheta
fugitivus*, fled touch, was in the transgression;
sent to Ninive and went to Joppe; sent east,
& went flat west: & was even taken with
the manner (as we say) and arrested in the
very flight. For an evill and an adulterous
generation, this was a good signe (say I:) and
so might they, if they knew their own good.
For them, and for us, and (in a word) for all
sinners; for he is *Propheta peccator*, and so
Propheta peccatorum. And Christ is pleased to
picke out His fugitive Prophet, His runaway,
and make him (a Sinner, and such a Sinner)
His Signe. As to come Himselfe in the
similitude of sinfull flesh; so, to make sinfull *Rom. 8. 3.*
flesh His similitude, to come into a *sicut*
with. All, that sinfull flesh might have hope
in the *Signatum*, in Him, of whom this was
the Signe. This, theirs, and ours.

The next is ours, and we highly to blesse *For us*, Prophe-
God for it: that being to set His signe in a ta gentium.
Prophet, He would doe it in him; choose him

out, to make him His patterne, who was
Propheta Gentium, the Prophet of the
Gentiles, sent to prophecie to Ninive, that
were heathen, as we and our fathers were.
And in that, a *Non nisi* too: For, none but he
was so: never a Prophet of them all, sent to
the heathen: the rest, to the Jewes, all. This
sending of his, to the Gentiles, was, to us of
the Gentiles, a gate of hope, that in former
ages, and long before Christ came in the
flesh, we Gentiles were not forgotten. Even
then, sent God a Prophet to Ninive. And
what was Ninive? the head Citie of the
Assyrians, the greatest Monarchie then in
being, and so the principall place of all
Paganisme. That thus, *in Signo*, we were not
forgotten, a signe it was, no more should we
be *in Signato*; but Christ be, to us, as Jonas
to them, a light to lighten the Gentiles, and
His salvation to the uttermost parts of the
earth.

Let me add this yet more, to our comfort.
This Jonas, whom He thus sent on this
errand to the Gentiles, what was he? Of all
the Prophets, all, whose prophecies we have
remaining on record in the Bible, the foure
great, the twelve lesse, of them all, all the
sixteene, He was the first in time, Senior to
them all. Plaine by 2. Kings 14. that he
prophesied long before eny of them. For, it
is there said, that his prophesie came to passe,
in the daies of Jeroboam the Second, who
lived the same time with Uzzia in Juda. And,

Hos. 2. 15.

Luk. 2. 32.
Esay. 49. 6.

Primus Pro-
phetarum.

2. *Kings* 14. 25.

in Uzzia's time, the eldest of all the rest, did
but begin to prophesie. So, his was doon,
before theirs was begoon. Him, that was
thus first in the ranke of them all, did God
send to us Gentiles; to us first, before eny,
to the Jewes. A Signe, we were not last; nay
first in His care: in that, visited by Him first,
as to whom He sent the first of all the
sixteene. And, I may say to you, this was to
them an Item, as if God were now to turne
Gentile, as looking that way, having a minde
to them then, even in Jona's time; they to
come in shortly, and the Jewes to be shut
out: and that, as they had then prioritie *in
Signo*, so should they no lesse, *in Signato*;
and the fullnesse of the Gentiles come in, *Rom.* 11. 25.
before the conversion of the Jewes. This, to
us Sinners, to us Gentiles, to us Sinners of
the Gentiles, was *Salutare Signum*, a health-
full Signe, every way.

These three are put, on the by. In the
maine point of the Text, and of the time,
two more.   1.

He, and *non nisi*, none but he, had the *Jonas* Signum
honor to be a *piacularis hostia* (as it were) for, *As* piacularis
the casting him into the sea, served (in a hostia.
sort) as a kind of expiatorie sacrifice, as farr,
as to the temporall saving of the ship, he
sailed in. And therein, as a meet Signe he
expressed Him, whose death was (after) the
full and perfect expiation of the sinnes of the
whole world.   2.

Then againe Jonas, and *non nisi*, onely he *As* Propheta
                                                    redivivus.

was *propheta redivivus*; that, his peculiar, above them all. He the onely Prophet, that went downe into the deepe into the Whale's bellie and came forth againe alive. Dead he was not, but (*lege viventium*) after the law of the living, one throwen overboord, into the Sea in a tempest, to all intents, may be given for dead; and so (I dare say) all the mariners in the ship gave Jonas. That he came out againe alive, it was by speciall grace, not by course of nature. For, from the Whale's bellie he came (for all the world) as if one should have come out of his grave; risen againe.

Among the Jewes, it goes for currant, the Rabbines take it up one after another, that this Jonas was the Widow of Sarepta's sonne; the childe, whom Elias raised from death to life (1. *Reg.* 17.) If so: then well might he be a Signe; A Signe, dead in his cradle once: as good as dead in the Whale's bellie, now againe: In both, resembling Him, whose Signe he was, if both be true: But, one is most certaine; and, to that, we hold us. And this is (indeed) the maine *Sicut*, the *Sicut* of the Text, and of the Day.

One more, and I have done; and that is, of the time: precise three dayes and three nights. For, in this a *Non nisi*. For, none but he, so: just three, neither more nor lesse. For, I aske, why not the signe of Joseph, or of Daniel? ª Joseph was in the dungeon, among condemned persons to die: ᵇ Daniel, in

1. Reg. 17. 23.

3.
As, three daies & three nights, in the Whales belly.

ªGen. 39. 20.
ᵇDan. 6. 16.

the lion's den, as deadly a place, as the Whale's bellie: yet, neither of them, made the signe of Christ. Why? Joseph was in his dungeon too long: Daniel, too short, but a night; not long enough, to represent Christ being in his grave. Onely Jona's time, just. And the time is it, heere. Els might the others have beene his Signe well enough, for the matter, if that had beene all.

But, the time is still stood on, and the daies numbred: that His Disciples, that all might know, how long, He would be from them, and not a day longer. And this, not without good cause. This day, was but the third day: and, this day, they were at *sperabamus*, did Luk. 24. 21. hope; did, but (now) doe not; their hope was fallen into a tertian: that, it was time, He were up againe. This Signe set, that they might know for a surety, by this day at the fardest, they should heare of Him againe.

Of which three. To verifie His being there three dayes, it is enough, if He were there but a part of every one of them: for, it is not three whole daies. As, in common phrase of speech, we say, the Sun shone, or it rained these three daies past, though it did not so, all day long, but some part onely of each. And if it rained at all, in every of them, we say true: It is enough. And so heere, the first day of the three, Jonas was in the ship, and Christ on the Crosse, till friday, some-what before the Sun-sett. All the second day,

Jonas was in the Whale, Christ in His Sepulcher. The third day, Jonas came out of the Whale, and Christ out of His grave, as it might be about the Sun-rising; for, this day, both Sunnes rose together.

To verifie the three nights: that doe we, reckoning as did the Jewes (and that, by *Gen.* 1. 5. 8. *&c.* warrant out of the Gen. 1.) the evening and the morning but for one; so, drawing still the precedent night, and compting it with the succeeding day. So doe they still: the night past, with the day following, as (in Genesis) they are taught; and we doing so, it will fall out right.

The Sicut *of* *these three daies.* To the *Sicut* then, of these three daies. There is in each of them, set downe a severall state of Jonas; and so of Christ. [1]Their going thither: [2]Their being there: [3]And their comming thence.

[1]*In their going* *thither.* *Good friday.* *Jon.* 1. 4. 5. Thus fell it the first day: Jonas was at sea, in a ship: A great tempest came; so great, as the ship was upon casting away.

Of tempests, some are of course, have their causes in nature; and, in them, art and strength will doe good. With Jonas (heere) it did not prevaile a whit. Thereby, they knew it to be one out of course, of God's immediate sending.

[Jon. 1.] 7. God sends not such tempests, but He is angrie. He is not angrie, but with sinne. Some great Sinner then, there is in the ship, and if the ship were well ridd of him, all would be calme againe.

To lotts they went: Jonas was found to be the partie.

Being found, rather then all should be cast away, he bid franckly, *Tollite me*, & *Jon. 1. 12.* *projicite*, Take me, cast me into the Sea.

Cast in he was, and the storme ceased 15. streight, the ship came safe home. And the Evening and the morning were the first day.

Will ye see now, what was acted in Jonas, actually fulfilled, in Christ? But (first) will ye note, that what is (in the Old Testament) written of Jonas, is not onely *historia vera*, but *Sacramentum magnum*, not a bare Storie onely, but besides the storie, pregnant also with a great Mysterie. Not onely, a deed *Ephes. 5. 32.* done, but further, a Signe of a deed to be done, of a farre higher nature; *Dico autem in Christo*, I speake it as of Christ and His Resurrection: Of that historie, this the Mysterie, this, the *Sacramentum magnum*.

Will ye note againe; it is on Christ's side with advantage. *Sicut Jonas* (saith this verse) But *ecce plus quàm Jonas* (saith the next;) and *Verse 41.* both may stand; There may be a *Sicut*, where yet there may be a *plus quàm*; a like-nesse in qualitie, where an exceeding in degree, though. Indeed, *Sicut* makes not a *non nisi*; *Plus quàm* doth: and we then, so to remember the *Sicut* in this, as we forget not the *Plus quàm*, in that. No more will we.

And now, weigh them over well, and whithersoever ye looke, ye shall finde a *plus quàm*. *Plus*, in the ship, in the tempest, in

the cause, in the danger, in the casting in, in
the comming out againe: In every one, a
plus quàm. All that was, in Jonas, in Christ
more conspicuous, and after a more excellent
manner; *in Signato*, then *in Signo*. That so,
in this, as in all els, Christ may have the
præeminence.

Col. i. 18.

To beginne then. It is no new thing to
resemble the Church, the Common-wealth,
yea the World, to a Ship. A Ship there was,
not a small barke of Joppe, but *plus quàm*, a
Great Arke, or Argosy, wherein were im-
barqued all Mankind, having their course
through the Maine Ocean of the world,
bound for the Port of Eternall blisse. And,
in this great Carrick, among the sonnes of
men, the Sonne of Man (as He termes
Himselfe) became also a passenger, even as
did Jonas, in his small bottome of Joppe.

Then rose there a tempest. A tempest it
selfe, and the cause of all tempests (the
heavy wrath of God, ready to seise upon
sinners) which made such a foule Sea, as this
great Ship, and all in it were upon the point
to be cast away. The *plus* (heere) is plaine:
take it, but as it was indeed litterally. For,
what a tempest was there at Christ's death!
It shooke the Temple, rent the veile, cleft the
stones, opened the graves, put out the Sunne's
light, was seene and felt all the world over;
as if heaven and earth would have gone together. But, the miserable storme, then,
who shall declare?

Chap. 27. 51.
52.

And, no mervaile: there was a great *Plus*, in the cause. For, if the sinne of one poore passenger (of Jonas) made such a foule Sea: the sinnes of the great Hulke, that bore in it all Mankind together in one bottome, what manner tempest (thinke you) were they like to raise? In what hazard, the vessell, that loaden with them all? But one fugitive, there: heere, all runne-awaies, from God, Master, Mariners, Passengers and all.

Now, the greater the Vessell, the more ever the danger. With Jonas, but a handfull like to miscarrie: In this, the whole masse of Mankind like to perish. So, in the perill, *Plus* too.

The storme will not be stayed neither, till some be cast into the Sea: and, some great Sinner it would be: And heer the *Sicut* seemes, as if it would not hold: heer, the only *Non Sicut Jonas*. For, Jonas there, was the onely sinner; all besides, in the ship, innocent poore men. Heere, Christ onely, in the ship, innocent, no sinner; all the ship besides, full fraught with sinners: Mariners, and Passengers, grievous sinners, all. Heere it seemes to halt.

And yet, I cannot tell you neither, for all that. For, in some sense, Christ was not unlike Jonas; no, not in this point: but, like Jonas, as in all other respects, so, in this too. Not, as considered in Himselfe; for so, he knew no sinne: But, Him that knew no 2. *Cor.* 5. 21. sinne, for us made He sinne: How? by laying *Esa.* 53. 6.

on Him the iniquities of us all, even of all the sonnes of men, upon this Sonne of Man. And, so considered, He is not onely *Sicut*, but *Plus quàm Jonas* heere. More sinne on Him, then on Jonas: for, on Him, the sinnes of the whole Ship, yea Jona's sinne and all.

For all that, heere is another *Plus*, though. For what Jonas suffered, it was for his owne sinne, and *meritò hæc patimur* might he say (and we both) with the Theefe on the Crosse. But Christ, what had He done? It was not, for his owne; it was, for other mens sinnes, He suffered, He paied the things he never tooke. So much the more likely was He, to satisfie; the just, for the unjust, the Lord, for the Servant: Much more, then if one sinner or servant should doe it for another.

Yet was Christ, as was Jonas, content to be throwen in. *Tollite me* (said Jonas;) *Sinite hos abire* (said Christ) Let these goe. Take me, my life shall answer for theirs; as it did. As content (said I?) Nay, *Plus* more. For, with Jonas, there was no other way, to stay the storme, but overboord with him. But, Christ had other waies; could have stayed it with His word, with His *Obmutesce*, as He did (the VIII. Chapter, before.) Needed not to have beene cast in: Yet, to fulfill all righteousnesse, condescended to it (though;) and in He was throwen, not of necessitie (as Jonas) but, *quia voluit*: and *Voluit, quia nos salvos voluit*, would have us safe, and His Father's justice safe, both.

Luk. 23. 41.

Psal. 69. 4.

1. *Pet.* 3. 18.

Jon. 1. 12.
Joh. 18. 8.

Cha. 8. 26.
Mat. 3. 15.
Esa. 53. 7.

Now to the effect. Therewith the storme stayed, God's wrath was appeased, Mankind saved: Heere, the *Plus* is evident. That of Jonas was but *Salus phaseli*, no more: This, was *Salus mundi*, no lesse. A poore boat, with the whole World, what comparison? And the evening and the morning were Good-friday, Christ's first day.

To Jonas, now, *secundò*: He was drowned *In their beeing there.* by the meanes. Nay; not so: God (before, *Easter Eve.* angry) was then pacified: Pacified, not onely with the ship, but pacified with Jonas too: provided a whale, in shew, to devoure him; indeed not to devoure, but to preserve him; downe he went into her belly.

There he was; but tooke no hurt there. 1. As safe, nay more safe there, then in the best ship of Tharsis: no flaw of weather, no foule sea could trouble him there. 2. As safe, and as safely carried to land: The ship could have done no more. So that upon the matter, he did but change his *vehiculum*; shifted but from one vessell to another; went on his way still. 3. On he went, as well, nay better then the ship would have carried him; went into the ship, the ship carried him wrong, out of his way cleane, to Tharsis-ward: Went into the whale, and the whale carried him right, landed him on the next shore to Ninive; whither (in truth) he was bound, and where his errand lay. 4. And all the while, at good ease, as in a cell or study; For, there, he indited a Psalme, expressing in it, his certaine hope of *Jon. 2. 2. 6.*

getting forth againe. So as, in effect, where he seemed to be in most danger, he was in greatest safety. Thus can God worke. And the evening and the morning, were Jona's second day.

The like now, in Christ: but still with a *plus quàm*. Doe but compare the whale's bellie, with the heart of the earth, and you shall finde, the whale that swallowed Christ (that is, the grave) was another manner whale, farr wider throated then that of Jonas. That Whale caught but one Prophet, but Jonas; This, hath swouped up Patriarchs, and Prophets and all; yea and Jonas himselfe too. None hath scaped the jawes of it.

And, more hard getting out (I am sure;) witnesse Jonas. Into the whale's belly he went, and thence he gat out againe. After he gat thence, into the heart of the earth he went, and thence he gat not: there he is still.

The Signe lyes, in this, by the letter of the Text. And, in Christ, the Signe greater. For, though to see a whale tumble with a Prophet in the bellie, were a strange sight: yet, more strange, to see the Sonne of God, lye dead in the earth: and, as strange againe, to see the Sonne of man, to rise from the grave againe, alone. A double signe in it.

The heart of the earth (with Justine Martyr, Chrysostome, Augustine) I take for the grave: though (I know) Origen, Nyssen, Theodoret take it for hell, for the place, where the Spirits are (as, in the bodie, that is

the place of them.) And, thither he went in
Spirit, & triumphed over the powers and *Col. 2. 15.*
principalities there, in His owne person. But
for His bodie, it was the day of rest, the last
Sabboth that ever was: and then His bodie
did rest, rest in hope, hope of what? that
neither His soule should be left in hell, nor
His flesh suffered to see corruption. For,
Christ had His psalme too, as well as Jonas.
David composed it for him long before (the
XVI. psalme, the psalme of the resurrection.) *Psal. 16. 10.*
And so the evening and the morning were
Christ's second day, Easter eve.

Now to Jona's *ultimò*. Jonas his hope *¹In their com-*
failed him not; the Whale's bellie, that *ming thence:*
Easter day.
seemed his toomb, proved his wombe, or
second birth-place. There he was: not, as
meat in the stomach; but, as an Embryo, in
the matrice of his mother. Strange! the
Whale to be as his mother, to be delivered of *Jon. 2. 10.*
him, and bring him forth into the world
againe. So, forth he came, and to Ninive   *3. 3.*
about his businesse. Thither he went, to
bring them out of the whale's bellie too. And
the evening and the morning were Jona's
third day.

Now the whale could not hold Jonas, no
more could the grave Christ, longer then this
morning, after breake of day: But, forth came
He too. And, with a *plus quàm*, in respect of
Jonas. It was in strict speech, with Jonas, no
resurrection: For, the truth is, he was never
dead: never he, but *putativè*. But, Christ was

dead, starke dead indeed, slaine outright
Joh. 19. 34   upon the crosse, His heart pierced, His heart
blood rann out. And, for dead taken downe,
Mat. 27. 66.   layd in, sealed up in His grave, a stone rolled
on Him, a watch set over Him. Made sure
(I trow) and yet rose for all that.

Another. Jonas rising, the whale gaped
wide, and streigned hard, and up came
Jonas. It was long of the whale, not of him or
Act. 2. 24.   any power of his. But, Christ, by His owne
power, broke the barrs of death, and loosed
the sorrowes of hell, of which it is impossible
He should be holden.

A third. Jonas rose but to the same state,
he was in before; but mortall Jonas still:
When he scaped, he drew his chaine after
him, and by the end of it was plucked back
againe afterward. But, Christ left them, and
linnen clothes and all, in the grave behind
Rom. 6. 9.   Him; rose to a better, to *ultra non morietur*,
never to die more, He.

And (in a word) the great *Plus quàm*. Jonas
was but *ejectus in aridam*: But, Christ was
receptus in gloriam. And, in signe of it, the
place whereon Jonas was cast, was drie land,
or cliffes, where nothing growes. The place,
wherein Christ rose, was a well-watered
garden, wherein, the ground was in all her
glorie, fresh and green, and full of flowers,
at the instant of His rising, this time of the
yeare. So, as He went lower, so He rose
higher, then ever did Jonas, with a great
Ecce plus quàm.

And yet, behold a greater then all these.
For, Jonas, when he came forth, came forth,
and there was all; left the whale, as he found
it. But, *Ecce plus quàm Jonas hîc, plus quàm* *Ver.* 41.
indeed. Christ slew the whale that devoured
Him, in the comming forth; was *mors mortis*:
He left not the grave, as He found it, but
altered the propertie, nay changed the very
nature of it, by His rising.

Three changes He made in it, very plainely.
1. Of a pit of perdition, which it was before,
He hath made it now an harbor of rest, Rest *Act.* 2. 26.
in hope. Hope of a new; not the same, it was
before, but a better farr, with a great *Plus
quàm*.

2. Made it againe (as the whale, to Jonas,
was) a convoy, or passing bote, to a better
Port, then any is in our Tharsis heer; even, to
the haven of happinesse, and heaven's blisse
without end. This for the soule.

3. And, for the body, made the grave, as a
womb for a second birth, to traveile with us
anew, and bring us forth to life everlasting;
Made *cor terræ ventrem ceti*, the heart of the
earth, to us, as the bellie of the whale was to
Jonas, which did not still reteine him. That,
did not him, nor this shall not us; shall not
hold us still, no more then the whale did him,
or the grave did Christ. There shalbe a
comming forth out of both. And, when God
shall speake to the earth (as to the whale He
did) the Sea and Grave both shall yield up *Apoc.* 20. 13.
their dead, and deliver them up alive again.

The very terme [of the heart of the earth] was well chosen. There is heart in it. For, if the earth have an heart, there is life in it; for, the heart is the fountaine of life, and the seate of the vitall spirits, that hold us in it. So, there is (we see:) for, the earth, dead for a time (all the winter) now, when the waters of heaven fall on it, shewes, it hath life, bringing forth hearbs and flowers againe. And, even so, when the waters above the heavens, and namely the dew of this day distilling from Christ's rising, shall in like sort drop upon it, it shalbe (saith Esai. Chap. XXVI.) as the dew of the herbs, and the earth shall give forth her dead. Dead men, as it doth dead plants now fresh and green againe, in the spring of the yeare. And so, the evening and the morning were Christ's third day, this day, Easter day morning.

Esa. 26. 19.

Thus many waies doth this *sicut* hold, and hold with a *plus quàm*. Were it not great pitie now, that Christ, who is so many waies *plus quàm Jonas*, for all this should come to be *minus quàm Jonas*, in this last, the chiefe of all? For, this is the chiefe. Jonas, after he came out of the whale, brought to passe that famous repentance the repentance of Ninive. At Jona's preaching, they repented at Ninive; at Christ's they did not, in Jerusalem.

Jon. 3. 5.

We shall mend this, if we be as the Ninivites; repent as they. As they? *Absit ut sic* (saith Saint Augustine; but adds then) *sed utinam vel sic*. As they? God forbid we

should be but, as they: As Christ was more
then Jonas, so Christians should be more then
Ninivites. Well, in the meane time, I would
we were, but as they; but so farr onward:
never plead for a *plus*, but be content with
Sicut, and never seeke more: But, that, we
must: For, lesse (sure) we cannot be. Christ
to be *plus quàm Jonas*, we to be *minus quàm
Ninivitæ*, it will not fit, it holds no propor-
tion.

The *Sicut* (ye see) and the *plus quàm*, both.
Now, what is the profitt of this Signe of the
Prophet? This Signe being of Christ's
giving, Christ gives no Signe, but it is
Signum in bonum, a Signe for good, a good
Signe; and a good signe is a signe of some
good. Of what good is this a Signe? Of hope
of comming forth (sure.) Comming forth,
whence? From a whale. What is meant by
the whale? (the deliverance (most-what) is, as
the whale is.) And, three whales we finde
heer: [1] Jona's whale: [2] Christ's whale: [3] and a
third: And, hope we have, to come forth of
all three.

First, Jona's whale; death it was not, it was
but danger; but, danger as neer death as
could be; never man, in more danger to
scape it, then he; if not in death, in *Zal-
maveth*, in the vale of the shadow of death, it
was.

Of any, that hath beene in extreme perill,
we use to say; he hath beene where Jonas
was; By Jona's going downe the whale's

*What this signe
portends.
Psal. 86. 17.*

Psal. 23. 4.

throat, by Him againe comming forth of the whale's mouth, we expresse, we even point out the greatest extremitie, and the greatest deliverance that can be. From any such danger, a deliverance is a kinde of resurrection, as the Apostle plainly speakes of Isaac, when the knife was at his throte, he was received *Heb.* 11. 19. from the dead ὡσεὶ ἐν παραβολῇ, though yet he did not. This for the feast of the Resurrection.

And thus, was Jonas a signe, to them of Ninive. As he scaped, so they: he his whale, they theirs (destruction:) which even gaped for them, as wide as Jona's whale. And, as to them a Signe, this; so, to us. And, this use we have of it; When at any time, we are hard bestead, this signe then to be set up for a token. And there is no danger so deadly, but we may hold fast our hope, if we set this signe before us, and say, What, we are not (yet) in the whale's belly; why, if we were there, from thence can God bring us though, as Jonas He did.

Jona's whale was but the shadow of death: Christ's, was death. And, even there, in death, to be set up. And we, no not in death *Job.* 13. 15. it selfe, to despaire, but (with Job) to say, yea though He kill me yet will I trust in Him. My breath, I may; my hope, I will not forgoe: *expirare possum, desperare non possum.* Heer now is our second hope: to come forth, to be delivered, from Christ's whale, from death it selfe.

But, if the whale be, or betoken the death of the bodie; it doth much more, the death of the soule. So shall we finde another whale yet, a third. And that whale is the red dragon, that great spirituall Liviathan, Satan. *Apoc.* 12. 3. And sin, the very jawes of this whale, that swoupeth downe the soule first, and then the bodie, and in the end both. Jonas had been deepe downe this whale's throte, before ever he came in the others: The land-whale had devoured him, before ever the Sea whale medled with him. In his flight, he fell into this land-whale's jawes, before ever the Sea-whale swallowed him up. And, when he had got out of the gorge of this ghostly Liviathan, the other bodily whale could not long hold him. And, from this third whale was Jonas sent, to deliver the Ninivites: which when he had, the other (of their temporall destruction) could do them no hurt. Their repentance ridd them of both whales, bodily and ghostly, at once.

Heer then is a third Cape of good hope: that, though one had been downe as deep in the entrailes of the spirituall great Liviathan, as ever was Jonas in the Sea-whale's, yet, even there also, not to despaire. He that brought Jonas, from the deepe of the Sea, and David from the deepe of the Earth *Psal.* 71. 20. (his bodie, so:) He also delivered his soule *Psal.* 86. 13. from the nethermost hell, where Jonas and He both were, while they were in the transgression.

And now, by this, are we come to the very Signature of this signe, even to Repentance, which followeth in the very next words, for they repented, at the preaching of Jonas. Jonas preached it: and (indeed) none so fit to preach on that theme (on repentance) as he, as one that hath been in the whale's bellie; in both the whale's, the spirituall whale's too (for Jonas had been, in both.) One that hath studied his sermon there, been in Satan's sive, well winnowed (*cribratus Theologus*) he will handle the point best; as being, not onely a preacher, but a Signe of repentance (as, Jonas was both) to the Ninivites.

Ver. 41.

And, as Jonas, so Christ: how soon He was risen, He gave order streight, that repentance (as the very vertue, the stamp of His resurrection) and, by it, remission of sins should be preached in His name to all nations.

Luc. 24. 47.

But (indeed) if you marke well, there is a neer alliance between the Resurrection and Repentance; reciprocall, as between the Signe, and the Signature. Repentance is nothing, but the soule's resurrection: Men are dead in sinne (saith the Apostle:) their soules are. From that death, there is a rising: Els were it wrong with us. That rising, is repenting: And when one hath lien dead in sinne long, and doth *eluctari*, wrastle out of a sinne, that hath long swallowed him up, he hath done as great a

Ephe. 2. 1.

masterie, as if (with Jonas) he had got out of
the whale's belly; Nay, as if (with Lazarus)
he had come out of the heart of the earth.
Ever holding this, that Marie Magdalen
raised from sinne, was no lesse a miracle,
then her brother raised from the dead.

And sure, Repentance is the very vertue of
Christ's Resurrection. There, it is first seen,
it first sheweth it selfe, hath his first opera-
tion, in the soule, to raise it.

This first being once wrought on the soule,
from the ghostly Liviathan, the like will not
faile, but be accomplished on the bodie,
from the other of death; of which Jonas is
heer, *Mysterium magnum, dico autem in* Ephe. 5. 32.
Christo. For, in Christ, this Signe is a
Signe, not betokening onely, but exhibiting
also what it betokeneth, as the Sacraments
doe. For, of Signes, some shew onely, and
worke nothing, such was that of Jonas, in it
selfe; *Sed Ecce plus quàm Jonas hîc*: For, Ver. 41.
some other there be, that shew and worke
both; worke what they shew, present us, with
what they represent; what they sett before us,
set or graft in us. Such is that of Christ.
For, besides that, it setts before us, of His:
it is further a seale or pledge, to us, of our
owne, that, what we see in Him this day,
shall be accomplished, in our owne selves, at
His good time.

And even so passe we to another Mysterie.
For, one Mysterie leads us to another: this
in the Text, to the holy Mysteries we are

providing to partake, which doe worke like, and doe worke to this: Even to the raising of the soule with the first resurrection. And, as they are a meanes for the raising of our soule, out of the soile of sin; (for, they are given us and we take them expressly for the remission of sinnes:) so are they no lesse a meanes also, for the raising our bodies out of the dust of death. The signe of that Bodie, which was thus in the heart of the earth, to bring us from thence, at the last. Our Saviour saith it *totidem verbis*, Who so eateth My Flesh and drinketh My Bloud, I will raise him up at the last day: raise him, whither He hath raised himselfe. Not to life onely, but to life and glorie, and both without end. To which &c.

Apoc. 20. 5.

Joh. 6. 54.

Lightning Source UK Ltd.
Milton Keynes UK
UKOW01f1040200218
318177UK00001B/7/P